The God of Carnage

Yasmina Reza is a French playwright and novelist, based in Paris, whose works have all been multi-award-winning, critical and popular international successes. Her plays, *Conversations After a Burial*, *The Passage of Winter*, *Art*, *The Unexpected Man*, *Life x 3* and *A Spanish Play*, have been produced worldwide and translated into thirty-five languages. Her new play, *Le Dieu du Carnage*, opened on 8 December 2006 at the Schauspielhaus in Zurich, directed by Jürgen Gosch, and in Paris on 25 January 2008 at the Théâtre Antoine, directed by the author, with Isabelle Huppert. Novels include: *Hammerklavier*, *Une Desolation*, *Adam Haberberg*, *Dans la Luge d'Arthur Schopenhauer*, *Nulle Part* and *L'Aube le Soir ou la Nuit*. Film includes: *Le Pique-Nique de Lulu Kreutz* directed by Didier Martiny.

Christopher Hampton was born in the Azores in 1946. He wrote his first play, *When Did You Last See My Mother?*, at the age of eighteen. His work for the theatre and cinema includes *The Philanthropist*, *Savages*, *Treats*, *Tales from Hollywood*, *The Talking Cure*, translations from Ibsen, Horváth, Molière and Chekhov, and the screenplays *Dangerous Liaisons*, *Total Eclipse*, *The Quiet American*, *Atonement*, *Carrington*, *The Secret Agent* and *Imagining Argentina*, the last three of which he also directed.

D1502654

YASMINA REZA

The God of Carnage

translated by
Christopher Hampton

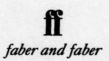

faber and faber

First published in 2008
by Faber and Faber Limited
3 Queen Square, London WCIN 3AU

Typeset by Country Setting, Kingsdown, Kent CT14 8ES
Printed in the United States by Quebecor World

© Yasmina Reza, 2008
Translation © Yasmina Reza and Christopher Hampton, 2008

Yasmina Reza and Christopher Hampton are hereby
identified as translators of this work in accordance with
Section 77 of the Copyright, Designs and Patents Act 1988

A CIP record for this book
is available from the British Library

ISBN 978-0-571-24258-0

10 9

The God of Carnage was first presented at the Gielgud Theatre, London, on 8 March 2008. The cast was as follows:

Alain Reille Ralph Fiennes
Annette Reille Tamsin Greig
Véronique Vallon Janet McTeer
Michel Vallon Ken Stott

Director Matthew Warchus
Designer Mark Thompson
Lighting Designer Hugh Vanstone
Music Gary Yershon
Sound Simon Baker
Producers David Pugh and Dafydd Rogers

Characters

Véronique Vallon
Michel Vallon
Annette Reille
Alain Reille

All are in their forties

THE GOD OF CARNAGE

*A living room. No realism.
Nothing superfluous.*

The Vallons and the Reilles, sitting down, facing one another. We need to sense right away that the place belongs to the Vallons and that the two couples have just met.

In the centre, a coffee table, covered with art books. Two big bunches of tulips in vases.

The prevailing mood is serious, friendly and tolerant.

Véronique So, this is our statement – you'll be doing your own, of course . . . 'At 5.30 p.m. on the 3rd November, in Aspirant Dunant Gardens, following a verbal altercation, Ferdinand Reille, eleven, armed with a stick, struck our son, Bruno Vallon, in the face. This action resulted in, apart from a swelling of the upper lip, the breaking of two incisors, including injury to the nerve in the right incisor.'

Alain Armed?

Véronique Armed? You don't like 'armed' – what shall we say, Michel, furnished, equipped, furnished with a stick, is that all right?

Alain Furnished, yes.

Michel 'Furnished with a stick'.

Véronique (*making the correction*) Furnished. The irony is, we've always regarded Aspirant Dunant Gardens as a haven of security, unlike the Montsouris Park.

Michel She's right. We've always said the Montsouris Park no, Aspirant Dunant Gardens yes.

Véronique Absolutely. Anyway, thank you for coming. There's nothing to be gained from getting stuck down some emotional cul-de-sac.

Annette We should be thanking you. We should.

Véronique I don't see that any thanks are necessary. Fortunately, there is still such a thing as the art of co-existence, is there not?

Alain Which the children don't appear to have mastered. At least, not ours!

Annette Yes, not ours! . . . What's going to happen to the tooth with the affected nerve? . . .

Véronique We don't know yet. They're being cautious about the prognosis. Apparently the nerve hasn't been totally exposed.

Michel Only a bit of it's been exposed.

Véronique Yes. Some of it's been exposed and some of it's still covered. That's why they've decided not to kill the nerve just yet.

Michel They're trying to give the tooth a chance.

Véronique Obviously it would be best to avoid endodontic surgery.

Annette Well, yes . . .

Véronique So there'll be an interim period while they give the nerve a chance to recover.

Michel In the meantime, they'll be giving him ceramic crowns.

Véronique Whatever happens, you can't have an implant before you're eighteen.

Michel No.

Véronique Permanent implants can't be fitted until you finish growing.

Annette Of course. I hope . . . I do hope it all works out.

Véronique Let's hope so.

Slight hiatus.

Annette Those tulips are gorgeous.

Véronique It's that little florist's in the Mouton-Duvernet Market. You know, the one right up the top.

Annette Oh, yes.

Véronique They come every morning direct from Holland, ten euros for a bunch of fifty.

Annette Oh, really!

Véronique You know, the one right up the top.

Annette Yes, yes.

Véronique You know he didn't want to identify Ferdinand.

Michel No, he didn't.

Véronique Impressive sight, that child, face bashed in, teeth missing, still refusing to talk.

Annette I can imagine.

Michel He also didn't want to identify him for fear of looking like a sneak in front of his friends; we have to be honest, Véronique, it was nothing more than bravado.

Véronique Of course, but bravado is a kind of courage, isn't it?

Annette That's right . . . So how . . . ? What I mean is, how did you find out Ferdinand's name? . . .

Véronique Well, we explained to Bruno he wasn't helping this child by shielding him.

Michel We said to him if this child thinks he can go on hitting people with impunity, why should he stop?

Véronique We said to him, if we were this boy's parents, we would definitely want to be told.

Annette Absolutely.

Alain Yes . . .

His mobile vibrates.

Excuse me . . .

He moves away from the group; as he talks, he pulls a newspaper out of his pocket.

. . . Yes, Maurice, thanks for calling back. Right, in today's *Le Monde*, let me read it to you . . . 'According to a paper published in the *Lancet* and taken up yesterday in the *FT*, two Australian researchers have revealed the neurological side-effects of Antril, a hypertensive beta-blocker, manufactured at the Verenz-Pharma laboratories. These side-effects range from hearing loss to ataxia . . .' So who the hell is your media watchdog? . . . Yes, it's very bloody inconvenient . . . No, what's most inconvenient about it as far as I'm concerned is the AGM's in two weeks. Do you have an insurance contingency to cover litigation? . . . OK . . . Oh, and Maurice, Maurice, ask your DOC to find out if this story shows up anywhere else . . . Call me back.

He hangs up.

. . . Excuse me.

Michel So you're . . .

Alain A lawyer.

Annette What about you?

Michel Me, I have a wholesale company, household goods, and Véronique's a writer and works part-time in an art-history bookshop.

Annette A writer?

Véronique I contributed to a collection on the civilisation of Sheba, based on the excavations that were restarted at the end of the Ethiopian–Eritrean war. And I have a book coming out in January on the Darfur tragedy.

Annette So you specialise in Africa.

Véronique I'm very interested in that part of the world.

Annette Do you have any other children?

Véronique Bruno has a nine-year-old sister, Camille. Who's furious with her father because last night her father got rid of the hamster.

Annette You got rid of the hamster?

Michel Yes. That hamster made the most appalling racket all night. Then it spent the whole day fast asleep. Bruno was in a very bad way, he was driven crazy by the noise that hamster made. As for me, to tell you the truth, I've been wanting to get rid of it for ages, so I said to myself, right, that's it. I took it and put it out in the street. I thought they loved drains and gutters and so on, but not a bit of it, it just sat there paralysed on the pavement. Well, they're not domestic animals, they're not wild animals, I don't know where their natural habitat is. Dump them in the woods, they're probably just as unhappy. I don't know where you're meant to put them.

Annette You left it outside?

Véronique He left it there and tried to convince Camille it had run away. But she wasn't having it.

Alain And had the hamster vanished this morning?

Michel Vanished.

Véronique And you, what field are you in?

Annette I'm in wealth-management.

Véronique Is it at all possible – forgive me for putting the question so bluntly – that Ferdinand might apologise to Bruno?

Alain It'd be good if they talked.

Annette He has to apologise, Alain. He has to tell him he's sorry.

Alain Yes, yes. Of course.

Véronique But is he sorry?

Alain He realises what he's done. He just doesn't understand the implications. He's eleven.

Véronique If you're eleven, you're not a baby any more.

Michel You're not an adult either! We haven't offered you anything – coffee, tea, is there any of that *clafoutis* left, Ronnie? It's an extraordinary *clafoutis*!

Alain I wouldn't mind an espresso.

Annette Just some water.

Michel (*to Véronique, on her way out*) Espresso for me too, darling, and bring the *clafoutis* anyway. (*After a hiatus.*) What I always say is, we're a lump of potter's clay and it's up to us to fashion something out of it. Perhaps it won't take shape till the very end. Who knows?

Annette Mm.

Michel You have to taste the *clafoutis*. Good *clafoutis* is an endangered species.

Annette You're right.

Alain What is it you sell?

Michel Domestic hardware. Locks, doorknobs, soldering irons, all sorts of household goods, saucepans, frying pans . . .

Alain Money in that, is there?

Michel Well, you know, it's never exactly been a bonanza, it was pretty hard when we started. But provided I'm out there every day pushing my product, it rubs along. At least it's not seasonal, like textiles. Although we do sell a lot of *foie gras* pots in the run-up to Christmas!

Alain I'm sure . . .

Annette When you saw the hamster sitting there, paralysed, why didn't you bring it back home?

Michel Because I couldn't pick it up.

Annette You put it on the pavement.

Michel I took it out in its cage and sort of tipped it out. I just can't touch rodents.

Véronique comes back with a tray. Drinks and the clafoutis.

Véronique I don't know who put the *clafoutis* in the fridge. Monica puts everything in the fridge, she won't be told. What's Ferdinand said to you? Sugar?

Alain No, thanks. What's in the *clafoutis*?

Véronique Apples and pears.

Annette Apples and pears?

9

Véronique My own little recipe.

She cuts the clafoutis and distributes slices.

It's going to be too cold, shame.

Annette Apples and pears, this is a first.

Véronique Apples and pears, it's pretty textbook, but there's a trick to it.

Annette There is?

Véronique Pears need to be cut thicker than apples. Because pears cook faster than apples.

Annette Ah, of course.

Michel But she's not telling you the real secret.

Véronique Let them try it.

Alain Very good. It's very good.

Annette Tasty.

Véronique . . . Gingerbread crumbs!

Annette Brilliant!

Véronique It's a version of the way they make *clafoutis* in Picardy. To be quite honest, I got it from his mother.

Alain Gingerbread, delicious . . . Well, at least all this has given us a new recipe.

Véronique I'd have preferred it if it hadn't cost my son two teeth.

Alain Of course, that's what I meant.

Annette Strange way of expressing it.

Alain Not at all, I . . .

His mobile vibrates, he looks at the screen.

I have to take this . . . Yes, Maurice . . . No, no, don't
ask for right of reply, you'll only feed the controversy . . .
Are you insured? . . . Mm, mm . . . What are these
symptoms, what is ataxia? . . . What about on a
standard dose? . . . How long have you known about
this? . . . And all that time you never recalled it? . . .
What's the turnover? . . . Ah, yes. I see . . . Right.

*He hangs up and immediately dials another number,
scoffing clafoutis all the while.*

Annette Alain, do you mind joining us?

Alain Yes, yes, I'm coming . . . (*To the mobile.*) Serge? . . .
They've known about the risks for two years . . . An
internal report, but it didn't formally identify any
undesirable side-effects . . . No, they took no precautions,
they didn't insure, not a word about it in the annual
report . . . Impaired motor skills, stability problems, in
short you look permanently pissed . . . (*He laughs along
with his colleague.*) . . . Turnover, a hundred and fifty
million dollars . . . Blanket denial . . . Idiot wanted to
demand a right of reply. We certainly don't want a right
of reply – on the other hand if the story spreads we
could put out a press release, say it's disinformation put
about two weeks before the AGM. . . . He's going to call
me back . . . OK.

He hangs up.

Actually I hardly had any lunch.

Michel Help yourself, help yourself.

Alain Thanks. I'm incorrigible. What were we saying?

Véronique That it would have been nicer to meet under
different circumstances.

Alain Oh, yes, right.
So the *clafoutis*, it's your mother's?

Michel The recipe is my mother's, but Ronnie made this one.

Véronique Your mother doesn't mix pears and apples!

Michel No.

Véronique Poor thing has to have an operation.

Annette Really? What for?

Véronique Her knee.

Michel They're going to insert a rotatable prosthesis made of metal and polyethylene. She's wondering what's going to be left of it when she's cremated.

Véronique Don't be horrible.

Michel She refuses to be buried next to my father. She wants to be cremated and put next to her mother who's all on her own down south. Two urns, looking out to sea, trying to get a word in edgeways. Ha, ha! . . .

Smiles all round. Hiatus.

Annette We're very touched by your generosity. We appreciate the fact you're trying to calm the situation down rather than exacerbate it.

Véronique Frankly, it's the least we can do.

Michel Yes!

Annette Not at all. How many parents standing up for their children become infantile themselves? If Bruno had broken two of Ferdinand's teeth, I'm afraid Alain and I would have been a good deal more thin-skinned about it. I'm not certain we'd have been so broad-minded.

Michel Course you would!

Alain She's right. By no means certain.

Michel Oh, yes. Because we all know very well it might easily have been the other way round.

Hiatus.

Véronique So what does Ferdinand have to say about it? How does he view the situation?

Annette He's not saying much. I think he's still slightly in shock.

Véronique He understands that he's disfigured his playmate?

Alain No. No, he does not understand that he's disfigured his playmate.

Annette Why are you saying that? Ferdinand understands very well!

Alain He understands he's behaved like a thug, he does not understand that he's disfigured his playmate.

Véronique You don't care for the word, but the word is unfortunately accurate.

Alain My son has not disfigured your son.

Véronique Your son has disfigured my son. Come back at five and have a look at his mouth and teeth.

Michel Temporarily disfigured.

Alain The swelling on his lip will go down, and as for his teeth, take him to the best dentist – I'm prepared to chip in . . .

Michel That's what the insurance is for. What we'd like is for the boys to make up so that this sort of thing never happens again.

Annette Let's arrange a meeting.

Michel Yes. That's the answer.

Véronique Should we be there?

Alain They don't need to be coached. Just let them do it man to man.

Annette Man to man? Alain, don't be ridiculous. Having said that, we don't necessarily have to be there. It'd probably be better if we weren't, wouldn't it?

Véronique The question isn't whether we should be there or not. The question is, do they want to talk to one another, do they want to have a reckoning?

Michel Bruno wants to.

Véronique What about Ferdinand?

Annette It's no use asking his opinion.

Véronique But it has to come from him.

Annette Ferdinand has behaved like a hooligan, we're not interested in what mood he's in.

Véronique If Ferdinand is forced to meet Bruno in a punitive context, I can't see the results would be very positive.

Alain Madame, our son is a savage. To hope for any kind of spontaneous repentance would be fanciful. Right, I'm sorry, I have to get back to the office. You stay, Annette, you'll tell me what you've decided, I'm no use whichever way you cut it. Women always think you need a man, you need a father, as if they'd be the slightest use. Men are a dead weight, they're clumsy and maladjusted – oh, you can see a stretch of the overground metro, that's great!

Annette I'm really embarrassed, but I can't stay either . . . My husband has never exactly been a pushchair father!

Véronique What a pity. It's lovely, taking the baby for a walk. And it lasts such a short time. You always enjoyed taking care of the children, didn't you, Michel? You loved pushing the pushchair.

Michel Yes, I did.

Véronique So what have we decided?

Annette Could you come by the house with Bruno about seven-thirty?

Véronique Seven-thirty? . . . What do you think, Michel?

Michel Well . . . If I may . . .

Annette Go on.

Michel I rather think Ferdinand ought to come here.

Véronique Yes, I agree.

Michel I don't think it's for the victim to go traipsing around. *stands up*

Véronique That's right.

Alain Personally, I can't be anywhere at seven-thirty.

Annette Since you're no use, we won't be needing you.

Véronique All the same, it would be better if his father were here.

Alain's mobile vibrates.

Alain All right, but then it can't be this evening. Hello? . . . There's no mention of this in the executive report. And no risk has been formally established. There's no evidence . . .

He hangs up.

Véronique Tomorrow?

Alain I'm in The Hague tomorrow.

Véronique You're working in The Hague?

Alain I have a case at the International Criminal Court.

Annette The main thing is that the children speak to one another. I'll bring Ferdinand here at seven-thirty and we can leave them to have their reckoning. No? You don't look very convinced.

Véronique If Ferdinand is not made aware of his responsibilities, they'll just look at each other like a pair of china dogs, it'll be a catastrophe.

Alain What do you mean, madame? What do you mean, 'made aware of his responsibilities'?

Véronique I'm sure your son is not a savage.

Annette Of course Ferdinand isn't a savage.

Alain Yes, he is.

Annette Alain, this is absurd, why say something like that?

Alain He's a savage.

Michel How does he explain his behaviour?

Annette He doesn't want to discuss it.

Véronique But he ought to discuss it.

Alain He ought to do any number of things, madame. He ought to come here, he ought to discuss it, he ought to be sorry for it, clearly you have parenting skills that put us to shame, we hope to improve, but in the meantime, please bear with us.

Michel Now, now! This is idiotic. Don't let's end up like this!

Véronique I'm only thinking of him, I'm only thinking of Ferdinand.

Alain I got the message.

Annette Let's just sit down for another couple of minutes.

Michel Another drop of coffee?

Alain A coffee, OK.

Annette Then I'll have one too. Thanks.

Michel That's all right, Ronnie, I'll do it.

Hiatus. Annette delicately shuffles some of the numerous art books dispersed around the coffee table.

Annette I see you're a great art-lover.

Véronique Art. Photographs. To some extent it's my job.

Annette I adore Bacon.

Véronique Ah, yes, Bacon.

Annette (*turning the pages*) . . . Cruelty. Majesty.

Véronique Chaos. Balance.

Annette That's right . . .

Véronique Is Ferdinand interested in art?

Annette Not as much as he should be . . . What about your children?

Véronique We try. We try to fill the gaps in the educational system.

Annette Yes . . .

Véronique We try to make them read. To take them to concerts and exhibitions. We're eccentric enough to believe in the pacifying abilities of culture!

Annette And you're right . . .

Michel comes back with the coffee.

Michel *Clafoutis*, is it a cake or a tart? Serious question.
I was just thinking in the kitchen – *Linzertorte*, for
example, is that a tart? Come on, come on, you can't
leave that one little slice.

Véronique *Clafoutis* is a cake. The pastry's not rolled
out, it's mixed in with the fruit.

Alain You really are a cook.

Véronique I love it. The thing about cooking is you have
to love it. In my view, it's only the classic tart, that's to
say on a pastry base, that deserves to be called a tart.

Michel What about you, do you have other children?

Alain A son from my first marriage.

Michel I was wondering, not that it's at all important,
what started the quarrel. Bruno won't say a blind word
about it.

Annette Bruno refused to let Ferdinand join his gang.

Véronique Bruno has a gang?

Alain He also called Ferdinand a grass.

Véronique Did you know Bruno had a gang?

Michel No. Fantastic!

Véronique Why is it fantastic?

Michel Because I had my own gang.

Alain Me too.

Véronique And what does that entail?

Michel There are five or six kids devoted to you and
ready to sacrifice themselves. Like in *Spartacus*.

18

Alain Absolutely, like in *Spartacus*!

Véronique Who knows about Spartacus these days?

Alain They use a different model. Spiderman.

Véronique Anyway, clearly you know more than we do. Ferdinand hasn't been as silent as you led us to believe. And do we know why Bruno called him a grass? No, sorry, stupid, that's a stupid question. First of all, I couldn't care less, also it's beside the point.

Annette We can't get involved in children's quarrels.

Véronique And it's none of our business.

Annette No.

Véronique On the other hand, what is our business is what unfortunately happened. Violence is always our business.

Michel When I was leader of my gang, when I was twelve, I fought Didier Leglu, who was bigger than me, in single combat.

Véronique What are you talking about, Michel? What's that got to do with it?

Michel No, you're right, it's got nothing to do with it.

Véronique We're not discussing single combat. The children weren't fighting.

Michel I know, I know. I just suddenly had this memory.

Alain There's not that big a difference.

Véronique Oh, yes, there is. Excuse me, monsieur, there's a very big difference.

Michel There's a very big difference.

Alain What?

Michel With Didier Leglu, we'd agreed to have a fight.

Alain Did you beat the shit out of him?

Michel Up to a point.

Véronique Right, shall we forget Didier Leglu? Would you allow me to speak to Ferdinand?

Annette By all means!

Véronique I wouldn't want to do it without your permission.

Annette Speak to him. What could be more natural?

Alain Good luck.

Annette Stop it, Alain. I don't understand you.

Alain Madame thinks . . .

Véronique Véronique. This will work out better if we stop calling each other 'madame' and 'monsieur'.

Alain Véronique, you're motivated by an educational impulse, which is very sympathetic . . .

Véronique If you don't want me to speak to him, I won't speak to him.

Alain No, speak to him, read him the riot act, do what you like.

Véronique I don't understand why you don't seem to care about this.

Alain Madame . . .

Michel Véronique.

Alain Of course I care, Véronique, enormously. My son has injured another child . . .

Véronique On purpose.

Alain See, that's the kind of remark that puts my back up. Obviously, on purpose.

Véronique But that makes all the difference.

Alain The difference between what and what? That's what we're talking about. Our son picked up a stick and hit your son. That's why we're here, isn't it?

Annette This is pointless.

Michel Yes, she's right, this kind of argument is pointless.

Alain Why do you feel the need to slip in 'on purpose'? What kind of message is that supposed to be sending me?

Annette Listen, we're on a slippery slope, my husband is desperate about all sorts of other things. I'll come back this evening with Ferdinand and we'll let things sort themselves out naturally.

Alain I'm not in the least desperate.

Annette Well, I am.

Michel There's nothing to be desperate about.

Annette Yes, there is.

Alain's mobile vibrates.

Alain Don't make any statement . . . No comment . . . No, of course you mustn't take it off the market! If you take it off the market, you become responsible . . . The minute you take Antril off the market, you're admitting liability! There's nothing in the annual accounts. If you want to be sued for falsifying the executive report and given the elbow in two weeks' time, take it off the market . . .

Véronique Last year, on Open Day, wasn't it Ferdinand who played Monsieur de . . .?

21

Annette Monsieur de Pourceaugnac.

Véronique Monsieur de Pourceaugnac.

Alain We'll think about the victims later, Maurice . . .
Let's see what the shares do after the AGM . . .

Véronique He was extraordinary.

Annette Yes . . .

Alain We are not going to take the medicine off the
market just because two or three people are bumping
into the furniture! . . . Don't make any statements for the
time being . . . Yes. I'll call you back . . .

He cuts him off and phones his colleague.

Véronique I remember him very clearly in *Monsieur de
Pourceaugnac*. Do you remember him, Michel?

Michel Yes, yes . . .

Véronique He was hilarious when he was in drag.

Annette Yes . . .

Alain (*to his colleague*) . . . They're panicking, they've
got the media up their arse, you have to prepare a press
release, not something defensive, not at all, on the
contrary, go out all guns blazing, you insist that Verenz-
Pharma is the victim of a destabilisation attempt two
weeks before its Annual General Meeting, where does
this paper come from, why should it have fallen out
of the sky just now, etcetera and so on . . . Don't say
anything about health problems, just ask one question:
who's behind this report? . . . Right.

He hangs up. Brief hiatus.

Michel They're terrible, these pharmaceutical companies.
Profit, profit, profit.

Alain You're not supposed to be listening to my conversation.

Michel You're not obliged to have it in front of me.

Alain Yes, I am. I'm absolutely obliged to have it here. Not my choice, I can assure you.

Michel They dump any old crap on you without giving it a second thought.

Alain In the therapeutic field, every advance brings with it risk as well as benefit.

Michel Yes, I understand that. All the same. Funny job you've got.

Alain Meaning?

Véronique Michel, this is nothing to do with us.

Michel Funny job.

Alain And what is it you do?

Michel I have an ordinary job.

Alain What is an ordinary job?

Michel I told you, I sell saucepans.

Alain And doorknobs.

Michel And toilet fittings. Loads of other things.

Alain Ah, toilet fittings. Now we're talking. That's really interesting.

Annette Alain.

Alain It's really interesting. I'm interested in toilet fittings.

Michel Why shouldn't you be?

Alain How many types are there?

Michel Two different systems. Push-button or overhead flush.

Alain I see.

Michel Depending on the feed.

Alain Well, yes.

Michel Either the water comes down from above or up from under.

Alain Yes.

Michel I could introduce you to one of my warehousemen who specialises in this kind of thing, if you like. You'd have to leg it out to Saint-Denis la Plaine.

Alain You seem to be very much on top of the subject.

Véronique Are you intending to punish Ferdinand in any way? You can carry on with the plumbing in some more appropriate setting.

Annette I'm not feeling well.

Véronique What's the matter?

Alain Yes, you're very pale, sweetheart.

Michel Palish, certainly.

Annette I feel sick.

Véronique Sick? . . . I have some Moxalon . . .

Annette No, no . . . It'll be all right . . .

Véronique What could we . . .? Coke. Coke's very good.

She immediately sets off in search of it.

Annette It'll be all right . . .

Michel Walk around a bit. Take a few steps.

She takes a few steps. Véronique comes back with the Coca-Cola.

Annette Really? You think so? . . .

Véronique Yes, yes. Small sips.

Annette Thank you . . .

Alain has discreetly called his office.

Alain . . . Give me Serge, will you, please? . . . Oh, right . . . Ask him to call me back, ask him to call me back right away . . .

He hangs up.

It's good, is it, Coca-Cola? I thought it was just supposed to be for diarrhoea.

Véronique Not only for that. (*To Annette.*) All right?

Annette All right . . . Véronique, if we want to reprimand our child, we'll do it in our own way and without having to account to anybody.

Michel Absolutely.

Véronique What do you mean, 'absolutely', Michel?

Michel They can do whatever they like with their son, it's their prerogative.

Véronique I don't think so.

Michel What do you mean, you don't think so, Ronnie?

Véronique I don't think it is their prerogative.

Alain Really? Explain.

His mobile vibrates.

I'm sorry . . . (*To his colleague.*) Excellent . . . But don't forget, nothing's been proved, there's nothing definite . . .

25

Get this straight, if anyone fucks up, Maurice is a dead man in two weeks, and us with him.

Annette That's enough, Alain! That's enough now with the mobile! Will you pay attention to what's going on here, shit!

Alain Yes . . . Call me back and read it to me.

He hangs up.

What's the matter with you, have you gone mad, shouting like that? Serge heard everything.

Annette Good! Drives me mad, that mobile, endlessly!

Alain Listen, Annette, I'm already doing you a big favour being here in the first place . . .

Véronique Extraordinary thing to say.

Annette I'm going to throw up.

Alain No, you're not, you are not going to throw up.

Annette Yes, I am . . .

Michel Do you want to go to the lavatory?

Annette (*to Alain*) No one's forcing you to stay.

Véronique No, no one's forcing him to stay.

Annette I'm feeling dizzy . . .

Alain Stare at a fixed point. Stare at a fixed point, Woof-woof.

Annette Go away, leave me alone.

Véronique She would be better off in the lavatory.

Alain Go to the lavatory. Go to the lavatory if you want to throw up.

Michel Give her some Moxalon.

Alain You don't suppose it could be the *clafoutis*?

Véronique It was made yesterday!

Annette (*to Alain*) Don't touch me! . . .

Alain Calm down, Woof-woof.

Michel Please, why get worked up about nothing?

Annette According to my husband, everything to do with house, school or garden is my department.

Alain No, it's not!

Annette Yes, it is. And I understand why. It's deathly, all that. It's deathly.

Véronique If it's so deathly, why have children in the first place?

Michel Maybe Ferdinand senses your lack of interest.

Annette What lack of interest?

Michel You just said . . .

Annette vomits violently. A brutal and catastrophic spray, part of which goes over Alain. The art books on the coffee table are likewise deluged.

Go and fetch a bowl, go and fetch a bowl!

Véronique runs out to look for a bowl and Michel hands her the coffee tray, just in case. Annette retches again, but nothing comes out.

Alain You should have gone to the lavatory, Woof-woof, this is ridiculous!

Michel Your suit's definitely copped it!

Very soon, Véronique is back with a basin and a cloth. The basin is given to Annette.

27

dérisif

Véronique Well, it's certainly not the *clafoutis*, it couldn't possibly be.

Michel It's not the *clafoutis*, it's nerves. This is pure nerves.

Véronique (*to Alain*) Would you like to clean up in the bathroom? Oh, no, the Kokoschka! Oh, my God!

Annette vomits bile into the basin.

Michel Give her some Moxalon.

Véronique Not now, she can't keep anything down.

Alain Where's the bathroom?

Véronique I'll show you.

Véronique and Alain leave.

Michel It's nerves. It's a panic attack. You're a mum, Annette. Whether you want to be or not. I understand why you feel desperate.

Annette Mmm.

Michel What I always say is, you can't control the things that control you.

Annette Mmm . . .

Michel With me, it's the cervical vertebrae. The vertebrae seize up.

Annette Mmm . . .

She brings up a little more bile. Véronique returns with another basin, containing a sponge.

Véronique What are we going to do about the Kokoschka?

Michel Well, I would spray it with Mr Clean . . . The problem is how to dry it . . . Or else you could sponge it down and put a bit of perfume on it.

Véronique Perfume?

Michel Use my Kouros, I never wear it.

Véronique It'll warp.

Michel We could run the hair-dryer over it and flatten it out under a pile of other books. Or iron it like they do with banknotes.

Véronique Oh, my God . . .

Annette I'll buy you another one.

Véronique You can't find it! It went out of print years ago!

Annette I'm terribly sorry . . .

Michel We'll salvage it. Let me do it, Ronnie.

She hands him the basin of water and the sponge, disgusted. Michel gets started on cleaning up the book.

Véronique It's a reprint of the catalogue from the '53 London exhibition, more than twenty years old! . . .

Michel Go and get the hair-dryer. And the Kouros. In the towel cupboard.

Véronique Her husband's in the bathroom.

Michel Well, he's not stark naked, is he?

She goes out as he continues to clean up.

. . . There, that's the worst of it. *The People of the Tundra* needs a bit of a wipe . . . I'll be back.

He goes out with the used basin. Véronique and Michel return more or less simultaneously. She has the bottle of perfume, he has the basin containing fresh water. Michel finishes cleaning up.

Véronique (*to Annette*) Feeling better?

Annette Yes . . .

Véronique Shall I spray?

Michel Where's the hair-dryer?

Véronique He's bringing it when he's finished with it.

Michel We'll wait for him. We'll put the Kouros on last thing.

Annette Can I use the bathroom as well?

Véronique Yes. Yes, yes. Of course.

Annette I can't tell you how sorry I am . . .

   Véronique takes her out and returns immediately.

Véronique What a nightmare! Horrible!

Michel Tell you what, he'd better not push me much further.

Véronique She's dreadful as well.

Michel Not as bad.

Véronique She's a phoney.

Michel Less irritating.

Véronique They're both dreadful! Why do you keep siding with them?

   She sprays the tulips.

Michel I don't keep siding with them, what are you talking about?

Véronique You keep vacillating, trying to play both ends against the middle.

Michel Not at all!

Véronique Yes, you do. Going on about your triumphs as a gang leader, telling them they're free to do whatever they like with their son when the child is a public menace – when a child's a public menace, it's everybody's concern, I can't believe she puked all over my books!

She sprays the Kokoschka.

Michel (*pointing*) Put some on *The People of the Tundra.*

Véronique If you think you're about to spew, you go to the proper place.

Michel . . . And the Foujita.

Véronique (*spraying everything*) This is disgusting.

Michel I was pushing it a bit with the shithouse systems.

Véronique You were brilliant.

Michel Good answers, don't you think?

Véronique Brilliant. The warehouseman was brilliant.

Michel What an arsehole. And what did he call her?! . . .

Véronique Woof-woof.

Michel That's right, 'Woof-woof'!

Véronique Woof-woof!

They both laugh. Alain returns, hair-dryer in hand.

Alain That's right, I call her Woof-woof.

Véronique Oh . . . I'm sorry, I didn't mean to be rude . . . It's so easy to make fun of other people's nicknames! What about us, what do we call each other, Michel? Far worse, isn't it?

Alain Were you wanting the hair-dryer?

Véronique Thank you.

Michel Thank you.

He takes the hair-dryer.

We call each other 'darjeeling', like the tea. Far more ridiculous, if you ask me!

Michel switches on the machine and starts drying the books. Véronique flattens out the damp pages.

Smooth them out, smooth them out.

Véronique (*as she smooths out the pages, raising her voice above the noise*) How's the poor thing feeling, better?

Alain Better.

Véronique I reacted very badly, I'm ashamed of myself.

Alain Not at all.

Véronique I just steamrollered her about my catalogue, I can't believe I did that.

Michel Turn the page. Stretch it out, stretch it out properly.

Alain You're going to tear it.

Véronique You're right . . . That's enough, Michel, it's dry. Objects can become ridiculously important, half the time you can't even remember why.

Michel shuts the catalogue and they both cover it with a little cairn of heavy books. Michel finishes drying the Foujita, The People of the Tundra, *etc. . . .*

Michel There we are! Good as new. Where does 'Woof-woof' come from?

Alain 'How much is that doggie in the window?'

Michel I know it! (*He sings.*) 'The one with the waggly tail.'

Alain 'Woof-woof.'

Michel Ha, ha! . . . Ours comes from our honeymoon in India. Idiotic, really!

Véronique Shouldn't I go and see how she is?

Michel Off you go, darjeeling.

Véronique Shall I? . . .

  Annette returns.

. . . Ah, Annette! I was worried about you . . . Are you feeling better?

Annette I think so.

Alain If you're not sure, stay away from the coffee table.

Annette I left the towel in the bathtub, I wasn't sure where to put it.

Véronique Perfect.

Annette You've cleaned it all up. I'm so sorry.

Michel Everything's great. Everything's in order.

Véronique Annette, forgive me, I've taken hardly any notice of you. I've been obsessed with my Kokoschka.

Annette Don't worry about it.

Véronique The way I reacted, very bad of me.

Annette Not at all . . . (*After an embarrassed hiatus.*) Something occurred to me in the bathroom . . .

Véronique Yes?

Annette Perhaps we skated too hastily over . . .
  I mean, what I mean is . . .

Michel Say it, Annette, say it.

Annette An insult is also a kind of assault.

Michel Of course it is.

Véronique Well, that depends, Michel.

Michel Yes, it depends.

Annette Ferdinand's never shown any signs of violence. He wouldn't have done that without a reason.

Alain He got called a grass!

His mobile vibrates.

I'm sorry! . . .

He moves to one side, making elaborately apologetic signs to Annette.

. . . Yes . . . As long as there aren't any statements from victims. We don't want any victims. I don't want you being quoted alongside victims! . . . A blanket denial and if necessary attack the newspaper . . . They'll fax you a draft of the press release, Maurice.

He hangs up.

If anyone calls me a grass, I'm liable to get annoyed.

Michel Unless it's true.

Alain What did you say?

Michel I mean, suppose it's justified?

Annette My son is a grass?

Michel Course not, I was joking.

Annette Yours is as well, if that's to be the way of it.

Michel What do you mean, ours is as well?

Annette Well, he did identify Ferdinand.

Michel Because we insisted!

Véronique Michel, this is completely beside the point.

Annette What's the difference? Whether you insisted or not, he gave you the name.

Alain Annette.

Annette Annette what? (*To Michel.*) You think my son is a grass?

Michel I don't think anything.

Annette Well, if you don't think anything, don't say anything. Stop making these insinuations.

Véronique Let's stay calm, Annette. Michel and I are making an effort to be reasonable and moderate . . .

Annette Not that moderate.

Véronique Oh, really? What do you mean?

Annette Moderate on the surface.

Alain I really have to go, Woof-woof . . .

Annette All right, go on, be a coward.

Alain Annette, right now I'm risking my most important client, so this responsible parent routine . . .

Véronique My son has lost two teeth. Two incisors.

Alain Yes, yes, I think we all got that.

Véronique One of them for good.

Alain He'll have new ones, we'll give him new ones! Better ones! It's not as if he's burst an eardrum!

Annette We're making a mistake not to take into account the origin of the problem.

Véronique There's no origin. There's just an eleven-year-old child hitting someone. With a stick.

Alain Armed with a stick.

Michel We withdrew that word.

Alain You withdrew it because we objected to it.

Michel We withdrew it without any protest.

 Alain A word deliberately designed to rule out error or clumsiness, to rule out childhood.

Véronique I'm not sure I'm able to take much more of this tone of voice.

Alain You and I have had trouble seeing eye to eye right from the start.

Véronique There's nothing more detestable than to be attacked for something you yourself consider a mistake. The word 'armed' was inappropriate, so we changed it. Although, if you stick to the strict definition of the word, its use is far from inaccurate.

Annette Ferdinand was insulted and he reacted. If I'm attacked, I defend myself, especially if I find myself alone, confronted by a gang.

Michel Puking seems to have perked you up.

Annette Are you aware how crude that sounds?

Michel We're people of good will. All four of us, I'm sure. Why let these irritants, these pointless aggravations push us over the edge? . . .

Véronique Oh, Michel, that's enough! Let's stop beating about the bush. If all we are is moderate on the surface, let's forget it, shall we!

Michel No, no, I refuse to allow myself to slide down that slope.

Alain What slope?

Michel The deplorable slope those two little bastards have perched us on! There, I've said it!

Alain I'm not sure Ronnie has quite the same outlook.

Véronique Véronique!

Alain Sorry.

Véronique So Bruno's a little bastard now, is he, poor child. That's the last straw!

Alain Right, well, I really do have to leave you.

Annette Me too.

Véronique Go on, go, I give up.

The Vallon telephone rings.

Michel Hello? . . . Oh, Mum . . . No, no, we're with some friends, but tell me about it . . . Yes, do whatever the doctor wants you to do . . . They've given you Antril?! Wait a minute, Mum, wait a minute, don't go away . . . (*To Alain.*) Antril's your crap, isn't it? My mother's taking it!

Alain Thousands of people take it.

Michel You stop taking that stuff right now. Do you hear what I'm saying, Mum? Immediately . . . Don't argue, I'll explain later . . . Tell Dr Perolo I'm forbidding you to take it . . . Why luminous? . . . So that you can be seen? . . . That's completely ridiculous . . . All right, we'll talk about it later. Lots of love, Mum. I'll call you back.

He hangs up.

She's hired luminous crutches, so she doesn't get knocked down by a truck. As if someone in her condition would be strolling down the motorway in the middle of the night. They've given her Antril for her blood pressure.

Alain If she takes it and stays normal, I'll have her called as a witness. Didn't I have a scarf? Ah, there it is.

Michel I do not appreciate your cynicism. If my mother displays the most minor symptom, I'll be initiating a class action.

Alain Oh, that'll happen anyway.

Michel So I should hope.

Annette Goodbye, madame . . .

Véronique Behaving well gets you nowhere. Courtesy is a waste of time, it weakens you and undermines you . . .

Alain Right, come on, Annette, let's go, enough preaching and sermons for today.

Michel Go on, go. But can I just say one thing: having met you two, it's pretty clear that for what's-his-name, Ferdinand, there are mitigating circumstances.

Annette When you murdered that hamster . . .

Michel Murdered?!

Annette Yes.

Michel I murdered the hamster?!

Annette Yes. You've done your best to make us feel guilty, but your virtue went straight out the window once you decided to be a killer.

Michel I absolutely did not murder that hamster!

Annette Worse. You left it, shivering with terror, in a hostile environment. That poor hamster is bound to have been eaten by a dog or a rat.

*Couples keep
turning on each other*

Véronique It's true! That is true!

Michel What do you mean, 'that is true'?

Véronique It's true. What do you expect me to say? It's appalling what must have happened to that creature.

Michel I thought the hamster would be happy to be liberated. I thought it was going to run off down the gutter jumping for joy!

Véronique Well, it didn't.

Annette And you abandoned it.

Michel I can't touch those things! For fuck's sake, Ronnie, you know very well, I'm incapable of touching that whole species!

Véronique He has a phobia about rodents.

Michel That's right, I'm frightened of rodents, I'm terrified of snakes, anything close to the ground, I have absolutely no rapport with! So that's the end of it!

Alain (*to Véronique*) And you, why didn't you go out and look for it?

Véronique Because I had no idea what had happened! Michel didn't tell us, me and the children, that the hamster had escaped till the following morning. I went out immediately, immediately, I walked round the block, I even went down to the cellar.

Michel Véronique, I find it intolerable to be in the dock all of a sudden for this hamster saga that you've seen fit to reveal. It's a personal matter which is nobody else's business but ours and which has nothing to do with the present situation! And I find it incomprehensible to be called a killer! In my own home!

Véronique What's your home got to do with it?

Michel My home, the doors of which I have opened, the doors of which I have opened wide in a spirit of reconciliation, to people who ought to be grateful to me for it!

Alain It's wonderful the way you keep patting yourself on the back.

Annette Don't you feel any guilt?

Michel I feel no guilt whatsoever. I've always found that creature repulsive. I'm ecstatic that it's gone.

Véronique Michel, that is ridiculous.

Michel What's ridiculous? Have you gone crazy as well? Their son bashes up Bruno, and I get shat on because of a hamster?

Véronique You behaved very badly with that hamster, you can't deny it.

Michel Fuck the hamster!

Véronique You won't be able to say that to your daughter this evening.

Michel Bring her on! I'm not going to let myself be told how to behave by some nine-year-old bruiser.

Alain Hundred per cent behind you there.

Véronique Pathetic.

Michel Careful, Véronique, you be careful, I've been extremely restrained up to now, but I'm two inches away from crossing that line.

Annette And what about Bruno?

Michel What about Bruno?

Annette Isn't he upset?

Michel If you ask me, Bruno has other problems.

Véronique Bruno was less attached to Nibbles.

Michel Grotesque name as well!

Annette If you feel no guilt, why do you expect our son to feel any?

Michel Let me tell you this, I'm up to here with these idiotic discussions. We tried to be nice, we bought tulips, my wife passed me off as a lefty, but the truth is, I can't keep this up any more, I'm fundamentally uncouth.

Alain Aren't we all?

Véronique No. No. I'm sorry, we are not all fundamentally uncouth.

Alain Well, not you, obviously.

Véronique No, not me, thank the Lord.

Michel Not you, darjee, not you, you're a fully evolved woman, you're skid-resistant.

Véronique Why are you attacking me?

Michel I'm not attacking you. Quite the opposite.

Véronique Yes, you're attacking me, you know you are.

Michel You organised this little get-together, I just let myself be recruited . . .

Véronique You let yourself be recruited?

Michel Yes.

Véronique That's detestable.

Michel Not at all. You stand up for civilisation, that's completely to your credit.

Véronique Exactly, I'm standing up for civilisation! And it's lucky there are people prepared to do that! (*She's on* *the brink of tears.*) You think being fundamentally uncouth's a better idea?

Alain Come on now, come on . . .

Véronique (*as above*) Is it normal to criticise someone for not being fundamentally uncouth? . . .

Annette No one's saying that. No one's criticising you.

Véronique Yes, they are! . . .

She bursts into tears.

Alain No, they're not!

Véronique What were we supposed to do? Sue you? Not speak to one another and try to slaughter each other with insurance claims?

Michel Stop it, Ronnie . . .

Véronique Stop what?! . . .

Michel You've got things out of proportion . . .

Véronique I don't give a shit! You force yourself to rise above petty-mindedness . . . and you finish up humiliated and completely on your own . . .

Alain's mobile has vibrated.

Alain . . . Yes . . . 'Let them prove it!' . . . 'Prove it' . . . but if you ask me, best not to answer at all . . .

Michel We're always on our own! Everywhere! Who'd like a drop of rum?

Alain . . . Maurice, I'm in a meeting, I'll call you back from the office . . .

He cuts the line.

Véronique So there we are! I'm living with someone who's totally negative.

Alain Who's negative?

Michel I am.

Véronique This was the worst idea! We should never have arranged this meeting!

Michel I told you.

Véronique You told me?

Michel Yes.

Véronique You told me you didn't want to have this meeting?!

Michel I didn't think it was a good idea.

Annette It was a good idea . . .

Michel Oh, please! . . .

He raises the bottle of rum.

Anybody?

Véronique You told me it wasn't a good idea, Michel?!

Michel Think so.

Véronique You think so!

Alain Wouldn't mind a little drop.

Annette Didn't you have to go?

Alain I could manage a small glass, now we've got this far.

Michel pours a glass for Alain.

Véronique You look me in the eye and tell me we weren't in complete agreement about this!

Annette Calm down, Véronique, calm down, this is pointless . . .

Véronique Who stopped anyone touching the *clafoutis* this morning? Who said, 'Let's keep the rest of the *clafoutis* for the Reilles'?! Who said it?!

Alain That was nice.

Michel What's that got to do with it?

Véronique What do you mean, 'what's that got to do with it'?

Michel If you invite people, you invite people.

Véronique You're a liar, you're a liar! He's a liar!

Alain You know, speaking personally, my wife had to drag me here. When you're brought up with a kind of John Wayne-ish idea of virility, you don't want to settle this kind of problem with a lot of yakking.

Michel laughs.

Annette I thought your model was Spartacus.

Alain Same family.

Michel Analogous.

Véronique Analogous! Are there no lengths you won't go to to humiliate yourself, Michel?

Annette Obviously it was pointless dragging you here.

Alain What were you hoping for, Woof-woof? It's true, it's a ludicrous nickname – were you hoping for a glimpse of universal harmony? This rum is terrific.

Michel It is, isn't it? *Coeur de Chauffe*, fifteen years old, direct from Santa Rosa.

Véronique And the tulips, whose idea was that? I said it's a shame the tulips are finished, I didn't say rush down to Mouton-Duvernet at the crack of dawn.

Annette Don't work yourself up into this state, Véronique, it's crazy.

Véronique The tulips were his idea! Entirely his idea! Aren't we allowed a drink?

Annette Yes, Véronique, and I would like one too. By the way, it's quite amusing, someone descended from Spartacus and John Wayne who can't even pick up a mouse.

Michel Will you *shut up* about that hamster! Shut up! . . .

He gives Annette a glass of rum.

Véronique Ha, ha! You're right, it's laughable!

Annette What about her?

Michel I don't think she needs any.

Véronique Give me a drink, Michel.

Michel No.

Véronique Michel!

Michel No.

Véronique tries to snatch the bottle out of his hands. Michel resists.

Annette What's the matter with you, Michel?!

Michel All right, there you are, take it. Drink, drink, who cares?

Annette Is alcohol bad for you?

Véronique It's wonderful.

She slumps.

Alain Right . . . Well, I don't know . . .

Véronique (*to Alain*) . . . Listen, monsieur . . .

45

Annette Alain.

Véronique Alain, we're not exactly soul-mates, you and me, but, you see, I live with a man who's decided, once and for all, that life is second rate. It's very difficult living with a man who comforts himself with that thought, who doesn't want anything to change, who can't work up any enthusiasm about anything . . .

Michel He doesn't give a fuck. He doesn't give a fuck about any of that.

Véronique You have to believe . . . you have to believe in the possibility of improvement, don't you?

Michel He's the last person you should be telling all this.

Véronique I'll talk to who I like, for fuck's sake!

The telephone rings.

Michel Who the fuck's this now? . . . Yes, Mum . . . He's fine. I say he's fine, he's lost his teeth, but he's fine . . . Yes, he's in pain. He's in pain, but it'll pass. Mum, I'm busy, I'll call you back.

Annette He's still in pain?

Véronique No.

Annette Then why worry your mother?

Véronique He can't help himself. He always has to worry her.

Michel Right, that's enough, Véronique! What is this psychodrama?

Alain Véronique, are we ever interested in anything but ourselves? Of course we'd all like to believe in the possibility of improvement. Of which we could be the architect and which would be in no way self-serving. Does such a thing exist? Some people drag their feet, it's their strategy, others refuse to acknowledge the passing of time, and drive themselves demented – what difference does it make? People struggle until they're dead. Education, the miseries of the world . . . You're writing a book about Darfur, fine, I can understand you saying to yourself, right, I'm going to choose a massacre, what else does history consist of, and I'm going to write about it. You do what you can to save yourself.

Véronique I'm not writing the book to save myself. You haven't read it, you don't know what it's about.

Alain It makes no difference.

Hiatus.

Véronique Terrible stink of Kouros! . . .

Michel Ghastly.

Alain You certainly laid it on.

Annette I'm sorry.

Véronique Not your fault. I was the one spraying like a lunatic . . . Anyway, why can't we take things more lightly, why does everything always have to be so exhausting? . . .

Alain You think too much. Women think too much.

Annette There's an original remark, I bet that's thrown you for a loop.

Véronique 'Think too much', I don't know what that means. And I don't see the point of existence without some kind of moral conception of the world.

Michel See what I have to live with?

Véronique Shut up! Will you shut up?! I detest this pathetic complicity! You disgust me.

Michel Come on, have a sense of humour.

Véronique I don't have a sense of humour. And I have no intention of acquiring one.

Michel What I always say is, marriag: the most terrible ordeal God can inflict on you.

Annette Great.

Michel Marriage and children.

Annette There's no call for you to share your views with us, Michel. As a matter of fact, I find it slightly indecent.

Véronique That's not going to worry him.

Michel You mean you don't agree?

Annette These observations are irrelevant. Alain, say something.

Alain He's entitled to his opinions.

Annette Yes, but he doesn't have to broadcast them.

Alain Well, yes, perhaps . . .

Annette We don't give a damn about their marriage. We're here to settle a problem to do with our children, we don't give a damn about their marriage.

Alain Yes, but . . .

Annette But what? What do you mean?

Alain There's a connection.

Michel There's a connection! Of course there's a connection.

Véronique There's a connection between Bruno having his teeth broken and our marriage?!

Michel Obviously.

Annette We're not with you.

48

Michel Children consume and fracture our lives. Children drag us towards disaster, it's unavoidable. When you see those laughing couples casting off into the sea of matrimony, you say to yourself, they have no idea, poor things, they just have no idea, they're happy. No one tells you anything when you start out. I have an old school pal who's just about to have a child with his new girlfriend. I said to him, 'A child, at our age, are you insane?' The ten or a dozen good years left to us before we get cancer or a stroke, and you're going to bugger yourself up with some brat?

Annette You don't really believe what you're saying.

Véronique He does.

Michel Of course I believe it. Worse, even.

Véronique Yes.

Annette You're demeaning yourself, Michel.

Michel Is that right? Ha, ha!

Annette Stop crying, Véronique, you can see it only encourages him.

Michel (*to Alain, who's refilling his empty glass*) Help yourself, help yourself – exceptional, isn't it?

Alain Exceptional.

Michel Could I offer you a cigar? . . .

Véronique No, no cigars!

Alain Pity.

Annette You're not proposing to smoke a cigar, Alain!

Alain I shall do what I like, Annette, if I feel like accepting a cigar, I shall accept a cigar. If I'm not smoking, it's because I don't want to upset Véronique, who's

49

already completely lost it. She's right, stop snivelling, when a woman cries, a man is immediately provoked to the worst excesses. Added to which, Michel's point of view is, I'm sorry to say, entirely sound.

His mobile vibrates.

. . . Yes, Serge . . . Go ahead . . . Put Paris, the date . . . and the exact time . . .

Annette This is hideous!

Alain (*moving aside and muffling his voice to escape her fury*) . . . Whatever time you send it. It has to look piping hot straight out of the oven . . . No, not 'We're surprised'. 'We condemn'. 'Surprised' is feeble . . .

Annette This goes on from morning to night, from morning to night he's glued to that mobile! That mobile makes mincemeat of our lives!

Alain Er . . . Just a minute . . .

He covers the mobile.

Annette, this is very important! . . .

Annette It's always very important. Anything happening somewhere else is always more important.

Alain (*resuming*) Go ahead . . . Yes . . . Not 'procedure', 'manoeuvre'. 'A manoeuvre, timed for two weeks before the annual accounts,' etc. . . . .

Annette In the street, at dinner, he doesn't care where . . .

Alain A 'paper' in inverted commas! Put the word 'paper' in inverted commas . . .

Annette I'm not saying another word. Total surrender. I want to be sick again.

Michel Where's the basin?

Véronique I don't know.

Alain . . . You just have to quote me: 'This is simply a disgraceful attempt to manipulate share prices . . .'

Véronique Here it is. Go on, off you go.

Michel Ronnie . . .

Véronique Everything's all right. We're fully equipped.

Alain '. . . share prices and to undermine my client,' confirms Maître Reille, counsel for the Verenz-Pharma company' . . . AP, Reuters, general press, specialised press, Uncle Tom Cobley and all . . .

He hangs up.

Véronique She wants to throw up again.

Alain What's the matter with you?

Annette I'm touched by your concern.

Alain It's upsetting me!

Annette I am sorry. I must have misunderstood.

Alain Oh, Annette, please! Don't let us start now! Just because they're quarrelling, just because their marriage is fucked, doesn't mean we have to compete!

Véronique What right do you have to say our marriage is fucked? Who gave you permission?

Alain's mobile vibrates.

Alain . . . They just read it to me. We're sending it to you, Maurice . . . 'Manipulation', 'manipulate share prices.' It's on its way.

He hangs up.

. . . Wasn't me who said it, it was François.

Véronique Michel.

Alain Michel, sorry.

Véronique I forbid you to stand in any kind of judgement over our relationship.

Alain Then don't stand in judgement over my son.

Véronique That's got nothing to do with it! Your son injured ours!

Alain They're young, they're kids, kids have always given each other a good drubbing during break. It's a law of life.

Véronique No, no, it isn't!

Alain Course it is. You have to go through a kind of apprenticeship before violence gives way to what's right. Originally, let me remind you, might was right.

Véronique Possibly in prehistoric times. Not in our society.

Alain Our society? Explain 'society'.

Véronique You're exhausting me, these conversations are exhausting.

Alain You see, Véronique, I believe in the god of carnage. He has ruled, uninterruptedly, since the dawn of time. You're interested in Africa, aren't you? . . . (*To Annette, who retches.*) . . . Feeling bad?

Annette Don't worry about me.

Alain I am worried.

Annette Everything's fine.

Alain As a matter of fact, I just came back from the Congo. Over there, little boys are taught to kill when they're eight years old. During their childhood, they may kill hundreds of people, with a machete, with a 12.7, with a Kalashnikov, with a grenade launcher, so you'll understand that when my son picks up a bamboo rod, hits his playmate and breaks a tooth, or even two, in Aspirant Dunant Gardens, I'm likely to be less disposed than you to horror and indignation.

Véronique You're wrong.

Annette (*mocking*) 12.7! . . .

Alain Yes, that's what they're called.

Annette spits in the basin.

Michel Are you all right?

Annette . . . Perfectly.

Alain What's the matter with you? What's the matter with her?

Annette It's just bile! It's nothing!

Véronique Don't lecture me about Africa. I know all about Africa's martyrdom, I've been steeped in it for months . . .

Alain I don't doubt it. Anyway, the Prosecutor of the International Criminal Court has opened an inquiry on Darfur . . .

Véronique You think I don't know about that?

Michel Don't get her started on that! For God's sake!

Véronique throws herself at her husband and hits him several times, with an uncontrolled and irrational desperation. Alain pulls her off him.

Alain You know what, I'm starting to like you!

Véronique Well, I don't like you!

Michel She's a supporter of peace and stability in the world.

Véronique Shut up!

Annette retches. She picks up her glass of rum and lifts it to her mouth.

Michel Are you sure about that?

Annette Yes, yes, it'll do me good.

Véronique follows suit.

Véronique We're living in France. We're not living in Kinshasa! We're living in France according to the principles of Western society. What goes on in Aspirant Dunant Gardens reflects the values of Western society! Of which, if it's all the same to you, I am happy to be a member.

Michel Beating up your husband is one of those principles, is it?

Véronique Michel, this is going to end badly.

Alain She threw herself on you in such a frenzy. If I were you, I'd be rather touched.

Véronique I'll do it again in a minute.

Annette He's making fun of you, you do realise?

Véronique I don't give a shit.

Alain I'm not making fun, on the contrary. Morality decrees we should control our impulses, but sometimes it's good not to control them. You don't want to be singing 'Ave Maria' when you're fucking. Where can you find this rum?

Michel That vintage, I doubt you can.

Annette 12.7! Ha, ha! . . .

Véronique (*same tone*) 12.7, you're right!

Alain That's right. 12.7.

Annette Why can't you just say gun?

Alain Because 12.7 is correct. You don't just say gun.

Annette Who's this 'you'?

Alain That's enough, Annette. That's enough.

Annette The great warriors, like my husband, you have to give them some leeway, they have trouble working up an interest in local events.

Alain It's true.

Véronique I don't see why. I don't see why. We're citizens of the world. I don't see why we should give up the struggle just because it's on our doorstep.

Michel Oh, Ronnie! Do stop shoving these thoughts for the day down our throat.

Véronique I'm going to kill him.

Alain's mobile has vibrated.

Alain . . . Yes, all right, take out 'regrettable' . . . 'Crude'. 'A crude attempt to . . .' That's it . . .

Véronique She's right, this is becoming unbearable!

Alain . . . Otherwise he approves the rest? . . . Fine, fine. Very good.

He hangs up.

What were we saying? . . . 12.7 millimetre? . . .

Véronique I was saying, whether my husband likes it or not, that no one place is more important than another when it comes to exercising vigilance.

Alain Vigilance . . . well . . . Annette, it's ridiculous to drink, the state you're in.

Annette What state? On the contrary.

Alain Vigilance, it's an interesting idea . . .

His mobile. It's Serge.

. . . Yes, no, no interviews before the circulation of the press release.

Véronique That's it. I insist you break off this horrendous conversation!

Alain . . . Absolutely not . . . The shareholders won't give a fuck . . . Remind him, the shareholder is king . . .

Annette launches herself at Alain, snatches the mobile and, after a brief look-round to see where she can put it, shoves it into the vase of tulips.

Annette, what the . . .!

Annette So there.

Véronique Ha, ha! Well done!

Michel (*horrified*) Oh, my God!

Alain Are you completely insane? Fuck!!

He rushes towards the vase, but Michel, who has got in ahead of him, fishes out the dripping object.

Michel The hair-dryer! Where's the hair-dryer?

He finds it and turns it on at once, directing it towards the mobile.

Alain You need locking up, poor love! This is incomprehensible! . . . I had everything in there! . . . It's brand new, it took me hours to set up!

gender solidarity again

Michel (*to Annette, above the infernal din of the hair-dryer*) Really, I don't understand you. That was completely irresponsible.

Alain Everything's on there, my whole life . . .

Annette His whole life! . . .

Michel (*still fighting the noise*) Hang on, we might be able to fix it . . .

Alain No chance! It's fucked! . . .

Michel We'll take out the battery and the SIM-card. Can you open it?

Alain tries to open it with no conviction.

Alain I haven't a clue, I've only just got it.

Michel Let's have a look.

Alain It's fucked . . . And they think it's funny, they think it's funny! . . .

Michel (*opening it easily*) There we are.

He goes back on the offensive with the hair-dryer, having laid out the various parts.

You, Véronique, you at least could have the manners not to laugh at this!

Véronique (*laughing heartily*) My husband will have spent his entire afternoon blow-drying!

Annette Ha, ha, ha!

Annette makes no bones about helping herself to more rum. Michel, immune to finding any of this amusing, keeps busy, concentrating intently.
 For a moment, there's only the sound of the hair-dryer. Alain has slumped.

Alain Leave it, mate. Leave it. There's nothing to be done . . .

Michel finally switches off the hair-dryer.

Michel We'll have to wait a minute . . . (*Hiatus.*) You want to use our phone?

Alain gestures that he doesn't and that he couldn't care less.

I have to say . . .

Annette Yes, what is it you have to say, Michel?

Michel No . . . I really can't think what to say.

Annette Well, if you ask me, everyone's feeling fine. If you ask me, everyone's feeling better. (*Hiatus.*) . . . Everyone's much calmer, don't you think? . . . Men are so wedded to their gadgets . . . It belittles them . . . It takes away all their authority . . . A man needs to keep his hands free . . . If you ask me. Even an attaché case is enough to put me off. There was a man, once, I found really attractive, then I saw him with a square shoulder-bag, a man's shoulder-bag, but that was it. There's nothing worse than a shoulder-bag. Although there's also nothing worse than a mobile phone. A man ought to give the impression that he's alone . . . If you ask me. I mean, that he's capable of being alone . . . ! I also have a John Wayne-ish idea of virility. And what was it he had? A Colt .45. A device for creating a vacuum . . . A man who can't give the impression that he's a loner has no texture . . . So, Michel, are you happy? It is somewhat fractured, our little . . . What was it you said? . . . I've forgotten the word . . . but in the end . . . everyone's feeling more or less all right . . . If you ask me.

Michel I should probably warn you, rum drives you crazy.

Annette I've never felt more normal.

Michel Right.

Annette I'm starting to feel rather pleasantly serene.

Véronique Ha, ha! That's wonderful! . . . 'Rather pleasantly serene'.

Michel As for you, darjeeling, I fail to see what's to be gained by getting publicly pissed.

Véronique Get stuffed.

   Michel goes to fetch the cigar box.

Michel Choose one, Alain. Relax.

Véronique Cigars are not smoked in this house!

Michel Those are Hoyo, those are Monte Cristo Number 3 and Number 4.

Véronique You don't smoke in a house with an asthmatic child!

Annette Who's asthmatic?

Véronique Our son.

Michel Didn't stop you buying a fucking hamster.

Annette It's true, if somebody has asthma, keeping animals isn't recommended.

Michel Totally unrecommended!

Annette Even a goldfish can prove counter-productive.

Véronique Do I have to listen to this fatuous nonsense?

   She snatches the cigar box out of Michel's hands and
   slams it shut brutally.

I'm sorry, no doubt I'm the only one of us not feeling rather pleasantly serene. In fact, I've never been so unhappy. I think this is the unhappiest day of my life.

Michel Drinking always makes you unhappy.

Véronique Michel, every word that comes out of your mouth is destroying me. I don't drink. I drank a mouthful of this shitty rum you're waving about as if you were showing the congregation the Turin Shroud. I don't drink and I bitterly regret it, it'd be a relief to be able to take refuge in a little drop at every minor setback.

Annette My husband's unhappy as well. Look at him. Slumped. He looks as if someone's left him by the side of the road. I think it's the unhappiest day of his life too.

Alain Yes.

Annette I'm so sorry, Woof-woof.

Michel starts up the hair-dryer again, directing it at the various parts of the mobile.

Véronique Will you turn off the hair-dryer?! The thing is buggered.

The telephone rings.

Michel Yes! . . . Mum, I told you we were busy . . . Because it could kill you! That medication is poison! Someone's going to explain it to you . . .

He hands the receiver to Alain.

Tell her.

Alain Tell her what? . . .

Michel Everything you know about that crap you're peddling.

Alain . . . How are you, madame? . . .

Annette What can he tell her? He doesn't know the first thing about it!

Alain Yes . . . And does it hurt? . . . Of course. Well, the operation will fix that . . . And the other leg, I see. No, no I'm not an orthopaedist . . . (*Aside.*) She keeps calling me 'doctor' . . .

Annette Doctor, this is grotesque – hang up!

Alain But you . . . I mean to say, you're not having any problems with your balance? . . . Oh, no. Not at all. Not at all. Don't listen to any of that. All the same, it'd probably be just as well to stop taking it for the moment. Until . . . until you've had a chance to get quietly through your operation . . . Yes, you sound as if you're on very good form . . .

Michel snatches the receiver from him.

Michel All right, Mum, is that clear, stop taking the medication, why do you always have to argue, stop taking it, do what you're told, I'll call you back . . . Lots of love, love from us all.

He hangs up.

She's killing me. One pain in the arse after another!

Annette Right then, what have we decided? Shall I come back this evening with Ferdinand? No one seems to give a toss any more. All the same, I should point out, that's what we're here for.

Véronique Now I'm starting to feel sick. Where's the bowl?

Michel takes the bottle of rum out of Annette's reach.

Michel That'll do.

Annette To my mind, there are wrongs on both sides. That's it. Wrongs on both sides.

Véronique Are you serious?

Annette What?

Véronique Are you aware of what you're saying?

Annette I am. Yes.

Véronique Our son Bruno, to whom I was obliged to give two Extra Strength Nurofen last night, is in the wrong?

Annette He's not necessarily innocent.

Véronique Fuck off! I've had quite enough of you.

She grabs Annette's handbag and hurls it towards the door.

Fuck off!

Annette My handbag! . . . (*Like a little girl.*) Alain! . . .

Michel What's going on? They've slipped their trolley.

Annette (*gathering up her scattered possessions*) Alain, help! . . .

Véronique 'Alain, help!'

Annette Shut up! . . . She's broken my compact! And my atomiser! (*To Alain.*) Defend me, why aren't you defending me? . . .

Alain We're going.

He prepares to gather up the parts of his mobile.

Véronique It's not as if I'm strangling her!

Annette What have I done to you?

Véronique There are not wrongs on both sides! Don't mix up the victims and the executioners!

Annette Executioners!

Michel You're so full of shit, Véronique, all this simplistic claptrap, we're up to here with it!

Véronique I stand by everything I've said.

Michel Yes, yes, you stand by what you've said, you stand by what you've said, your infatuation for a bunch of Sudanese coons is bleeding into everything now.

Véronique I'm appalled. Why are you choosing to show yourself in this horrible light?

Michel Because I feel like it. I feel like showing myself in a horrible light.

Véronique One day you may understand the extreme gravity of what's going on in that part of the world and you'll be ashamed of this inertia and your repulsive nihilism.

Michel You're just wonderful, darjeeling, you're the best of us all!

Véronique I am. Yes.

Annette Let's get out of here, Alain, these people are monsters!

She drains her glass and goes to pick up the bottle.

Alain (*preventing her*) . . . Stop it, Annette.

Annette No, I want to drink some more, I want to get pissed out of my head, this bitch hurls my handbag across the room and no one bats an eyelid, I want to get drunk!

Alain You already are.

Annette Why are you letting them call my son an executioner? You come to their house to settle things and you get insulted and bullied and lectured on how to be a good citizen of the planet – our son did well to clout yours, and I wipe my arse with your charter of human rights!

Michel A mouthful of grog and, bam, the real face appears.

Véronique I told you! Didn't I tell you?

Alain What did you tell him?

Véronique That she was a phoney. This woman is a phoney. I'm sorry.

Annette (*upset*) Ha, ha, ha! . . .

Alain When did you tell him?

Véronique When you were in the bathroom.

Alain You'd known her for fifteen minutes but you could tell she was a phoney.

Véronique It's the kind of thing I pick up on right away.

Michel It's true.

Véronique I have an instinct for that kind of thing.

Alain And 'phoney', what does that mean?

Annette I don't want to hear any more! Why are you putting me through this, Alain?

Alain Calm down, Woof-woof.

Véronique She's someone who tries to round off corners. Full stop. She's all front. She doesn't care any more than you do.

Michel It's true.

Alain It's true.

Véronique 'It's true'! Are you saying it's true?

Michel They don't give a fuck! They haven't given a fuck since the start, it's obvious! Her too, you're right!

Alain And you do, I suppose? (*To Annette.*) Let me say something, love. (*To Michel.*) Explain to me in what way you care, Michel. What does the word mean in the first place? You're far more authentic when you're showing yourself in a horrible light. To tell the truth, no one in this room cares, except for Véronique, whose integrity, it has to be said, must be acknowledged.

Véronique Don't acknowledge me! Don't acknowledge me!

Annette I care. I absolutely care.

Alain We only care about our own feelings, Annette, we're not social crusaders, (*To Véronique.*) I saw your friend Jane Fonda on TV the other day, I was inches away from buying a Ku Klux Klan poster . . .

Véronique What do you mean, 'my friend'? What's Jane Fonda got to do with all this? . . .

Alain You're the same breed. You're part of the same category of woman – committed, problem-solving. That's not what we like about women, what we like about women is sensuality, wildness, hormones. Women who make a song and dance about their intuition, women who are custodians of the world depress us – even him, poor Michel, your husband, he's depressed . . .

Michel Don't speak for me!

Véronique Who gives a flying fuck what you like about women? Where does this lecture come from? A man like you, who could begin to give a fuck for your opinion?

Alain She's yelling. She's a regimental sergeant major.

Véronique What about her, doesn't she yell?! When she said that little bastard had done well to clout our son?

Annette Yes, he did do well! At least he's not a snivelling little poof!

Véronique Yours is a grass, is that any better?

Annette Alain, let's go! What are we doing, staying in this dump?

She makes to leave, then returns towards the tulips which she lashes out at violently. Flowers fly, disintegrate and scatter all over the place.

There, there, that's what I think of your pathetic flowers, your hideous tulips! . . . Ha, ha, ha! (*She bursts into tears.*) . . . It's the worst day of my life as well.

Silence.
A long stunned pause.
Michel picks something up off the floor.

Michel (*to Annette*) This yours?

Annette takes a spectacle case, opens it and takes out a pair of glasses.

Annette Thanks . . .

Michel Not broken? . . .

Annette No . . .

Hiatus.

Michel What I always say is . . .

Alain starts gathering up the stems and petals.

Leave it.

Alain No . . .

The telephone rings. After some hesitation, Véronique picks up the receiver.

Véronique Yes, darling . . . Oh, good . . . Will you be able to do your homework at Annabelle's? . . . No, no, darling, we haven't found her . . . Yes, I went all the way to the supermarket. But you know, my love, Nibbles is very resourceful, I think you have to have faith in her. You think she was happy in a cage? . . . Daddy's very sad, he didn't mean to upset you . . . Of course you will. Yes, of course you'll speak to him again. Listen, darling, we're worried enough already about your brother . . . She'll eat . . . she'll eat leaves . . . acorns, conkers . . . she'll find things, she knows what food she needs . . . Worms, snails, stuff that drops out of rubbish bins, she's like us, she's omnivorous . . . See you soon, sweetheart.

Hiatus.

Michel I dare say that creature's stuffing its face as we speak.

Véronique No.

Silence.

Michel What do we know?